# LEADER FOR LIFE

## LESSONS LEARNED AS A FORTUNE 500 EXECUTIVE, A NURSE, A WAITRESS, A TACO BELL MANAGER AND A MOM

# LEADER FOR LIFE

## LESSONS LEARNED AS A FORTUNE 500 EXECUTIVE, A NURSE, A WAITRESS, A TACO BELL MANAGER AND A MOM

*Cindy Barnard*

# *Dedication*

To my Posse - defined as the past and present special leaders of the Sierra Terrific Division, Dream Team and the Georgia Wave

To those who followed joyfully….

To those who followed cautiously or even begrudgingly…

To those who refused to follow…

I learned from each of you

I'm honored by the trust you bestowed

I'm in awe of the leaders so many of you have become

I'm inspired by the ripples you are creating

We are all Pebbles

# POSSE

Sean Maribel Kevin Helen
Merlie Suzy Neal
Pam Janice Valerie Darlene Tammy Georgia Suzzette Teji
Lina Joyce Jennifer Carolyn Evelyn Connie
Don Peter Matthew Mario
Christine Amy Ilene
Donna Kathy Michelle Lelani
Kendra Levi Agnes
Kim Arlene Theresa Delaine Mike
Lorrie Mely Margarita Patrick Linda
Karla Michael Jack Bryan
Paul Olivia Heather
Beulah Saira
John MaryFrances Vicky Tina
Emy Lee Lynne
Amber Mary Barbara
Scott Jon Sandra
Stephanie Carol
Jillia David Thaddeus Jeff
Susie Sukan Cathy Emily
Nessa Sharon Cheryl Melissa
Geri Doreen Kristian Naomi Debra
Karen Rachel Gayle Mark
Leti Faye Betty Jannette Laura Vicki

# Acknowledgment and Gratitude

**Kent Thiry** – for sharing your strength and weaknesses- for your support and protection through good times and bad. You have earned my unqualified respect, appreciation and allegiance.

**Sean Graham, Lorrie Soares and Heather Ashbaugh** –for leading my Posse- for being partners I can count on, friends I can laugh with, and continuing to exceed expectations. I am fulfilled by witnessing your growth and accomplishments and ever grateful for your loyalty.

**Theresa Deed-Williams**- for the precious gift of a loving friendship.

**Leslie Janzen and Teddie Lopez**, my daughter and son—for bringing me motivation and clarity of vision when you were born and joy beyond reason when you blessed me with my incredible grandchildren, **Jacob, Jack, and Merrill**.

**Lia Kim Parker**—for knowing all my flaws and remaining a true friend for life.

**Doug Barnard**, my brother—for your unwavering support, your amazing brain, and brutal honesty. I admire you beyond words.

**Donny Barnard**, my brother—for sharing your work ethic and solid spirit.

**Jimmy Barnard**, my oldest brother—for your persistence and leadership getting your giant foot in the door at Taco Bell in 1967, keeping us laughing for over fifty years, and for being one tough dude who was unwilling to be taken down by a silly thing like a massive brain tumor. We would have missed you.

**Wanda Jean**, my mother—for your relentless and unique brand of mothering. You are one of a kind, and I know get my strength and resilience from you.

**Robert Charles Mills**—for being the mate of my soul.

# Contents

# Introduction

Why write another book on leadership? After all, there are thousands of them in print already, most likely hundreds of thousands. What could I possibly add that hasn't been said already? The answer may well be only information seen through the filter of a fresh perspective. A change in perspective can be a catalyst for a powerful shift in point of view. Allow me to take a couple of steps back to provide some background information.

The idea for this manuscript was born one weekend in November 2008 at a Coaches Training Institute session in San Rafael, California. After a long career as an operating executive in the dialysis field, I made the change to leading a team of human resource professionals. As I approached the middle of my fifth decade it seemed like the right time to evaluate where my skills could make the biggest impact in what could be the last few years of my career. I've always gravitated to the people side of the business, and while I had a track record of leading a division of dialysis clinics with consistently solid clinical and financial outcomes, it was improving teammate engagement, satisfaction, and retention that called to me. Ultimately, People Services, that's HR in the language of DaVita, was the logical choice.

Since my training was in nursing and later business, I researched options to expand my skill set in the human resources arena. At the time DaVita was spending a lot of money on outside consultants who provided coaching to the executive team. I had personally benefitted from the investment and was fortunate to have been exposed to some of the best coaches in the industry like **Foster Mobley** and **Dede Henley**. My decision to make the change and ultimately be trained as a coach myself occurred during the period when I was working one on one with the amazing **Carol Zizzo**. I could never have anticipated the personal transformation set in motion, and I am truly grateful to **Dennis Kogod**, my boss at the time and now COO of DaVita, for his willingness to make the investment in me.

Anyone lucky enough to experience the Coaches Training Institute (CTI) program knows that while you are learning how to coach others, it is impossible to make it through without doing a lot of work on yourself. Even if you resist, it still happens, and in my case I was open to making the most of the experience. I found myself in a group of bright but young, aspiring coaches. There were multiple sessions each three days at a time. As the program continued I gained a lot of clarity about my place in the class and in the workplace. Instead of resisting my "elder" status I chose to embrace it. I realized that with age and experience comes wisdom. We worked back and forth practice coaching each other, but the issues were all real. I gained a lot from my fellow students and by observing the class interactions realized how much I knew about leadership. This is not intended as bragging or self-promotion. The realization emerged that my years in operations, the challenging consolidation of the dialysis industry, and the gift of exposure to top-level executives had provided me a high-quality, hands-on, educational experience. Add to that my early years as a waitress, a Taco Bell manager, and a nurse and I knew I had experienced a unique and richly diverse view of human behavior.

In the coaching environment, it's impossible to separate your work life from personal. We learn that it's all part of the brilliant tapestry of color and texture that makes us who we are at any given time. Many hours were spent in honest reflection. Digging deep, I found myself filled with a desire to document what I had learned over the years if only to share it with my children and grandchildren. I had a clear vision of writing down a few of the key things I knew for sure about leading people and teams. Nothing long-winded, just bottom line, to the point so what I knew wouldn't die with me. I had the urge to write. Would it be an article or essay or even more? I didn't know. I just started writing stuff down. My only criteria: it had to be things I knew for sure about leadership. As a matter of fact, that was my working title, "Things I Know for Sure."

In high school I'd toyed with the idea of a career in journalism but the reality of life and the need to make a living to support my children led me to health care. I enjoyed writing but never considered myself an author. This being my first full manuscript, I don't have a point of reference, but it's my perception that I started writing quickly. It was a clear and present urge to write—to just get the words on paper.

In the process of writing, the transformation continued. In July 2009 I volunteered to go on a medical mission to help open a dialysis clinic in a rural area of the Philippines. That experience led to a strong desire to use my skills to be of service resulting in another life-changing decision to move from People Services to be the operating director of Bridge of Life—DaVita Medical Missions. By the spring of 2010 I was working full-time for Bridge of Life. The transition from for profit to nonprofit was challenging, but I was fortunate to still be affiliated with DaVita. For the first time in over twenty years I did not have a direct report. A big adjustment, for sure, but stepping away from a direct leadership position created an ideal environment for reflecting on the journey. The desire to write did not subside, but time is still a precious resource to be allocated wisely and Bridge of Life was my priority, so progress slowed in 2010 while I adjusted to my new position. By the beginning of 2011 I was experiencing a good level of life balance, and I felt a renewed urge to write and began again in earnest.

I spent some time researching publishing options and formalizing the plan for what I wanted the book to be. (By this time I knew it would be more than an essay.) I've read many fine books on leadership. There *are* many fine books on leadership. I think about books like *Credibility* by James Kouzes and Barry Posner and *Swim with the Dolphins* by Connie Glaser and Barbara Steinberg Smalley. I read them cover to cover and learned a lot from them. They impacted my behavior and I recommended them to others.

Then I thought about *The Five Dysfunctions of a Team* and *Death by Meeting* by Patrick Lencioni and realized I had learned just as much from those, but the time investment was much less. I knew then I wanted to honor the time commitment of the reader so the book would be short and to the point. In nursing we use cheat sheets and handbooks. In business we use dashboards and checklists. Why not create that type of resource for leaders?

I present to you a short book I wish I'd had in my backpack thirty years ago but that is still relevant today. It is designed to be read in its entirety (perhaps on an airplane) but the topics can stand alone as a quick reference. Commonsense, reality-based leadership shared not by the acknowledged thought leaders of our time but from the viewpoint of an ordinary frontline leader who was blessed to be exposed to extraordinary people and events. I'm a lucky girl.

# *In the Beginning...*
# *This Really Happened*

My first management job was at Taco Bell in 1972. I had been working part-time for a couple of years while attending high school, and the owner was preparing to open a new location and planned to move my manager (who happened to be my brother, Donny) to the new store in a nearby town. I was seventeen, had graduated from high school a week before, and thought I could work full-time and attend the local junior college. Donny went to bat for me with Gary, the area manager, and got me an interview.

When I think back on the conversation now, it's pretty comical, but at the time I was stone-cold serious. He knew I was a hard worker, but they had never considered a "girl" manager before. He looked at me and said, "You know if you want to be a manager you are going to have to be a real bitch; otherwise they will walk all over you." I said, "Yes sir, I can do that, no problem," and I was in.

The lessons I learned from my Taco Bell experience were many. A teenager managing a group of teenagers is a situation ripe with opportunity for conflict, especially when the manager has this voice in her head saying, *Remember to be a bitch; don't let them get away with anything or they'll think you're weak.*

With the advantage and clarity of hindsight it's easy now to see the red flags. Working with family, hiring a bunch of my friends from Fresno High, being indignant at the insubordination (my first experience with that word), and being absolutely amazed that not everyone had the same work ethic as Donny and me. I thought the owner was incredibly generous to allow us free food when we were on duty so it was shocking to me that some of the people I hired actually stole money from the cash register. And though I made many mistakes along the way, I came to rule that place with an iron fist, and no one ever accused me of being weak.

I noticed two distinct groups of workers: those who came in cognizant of the fact that they were being paid to work (OK, it may have only been a student wage of $1.40 per hour but it seemed like a lot at the time) and those who tried to get away with doing as little as possible counting the minutes until they could leave. Some would say if we paid more, we would have attracted better workers, but I've come to believe that's not true.

The willingness and drive to work an honest day for an honest dollar comes from a foundation of core beliefs and values. Values are not set in stone at the age of seventeen, but work habits exhibited on a job considered a stop-off point on the way to a "real" job will inevitably show up later in the workplace. This is true for all ages and income levels. I so appreciate my foundation, especially the gift of working with my brother who was my role model in all areas of work and integrity.

During the many years of my professional growth and development I came to see that my best decisions were made utilizing both my head and heart. Choosing the right thing to do and making decisions for the right reason are essential components for all functions of leadership. Whether dealing with personal or professional challenges, we all face leadership decisions every day of our lives and call upon our values and experience to guide us through the journey. And indeed, it is a journey worth taking.

"Your job gives you authority. Your behavior gives you respect."

—Irwin Federman

# *Leaders Require Followers*

It's amazing how many people believe they are leaders simply by virtue of their job title. Your position in an organization can only get you so far. True leadership occurs when individuals willingly choose to follow, not because it is required or demanded. Our beliefs drive our behavior. People observe the behavior of their leader and are inspired to change what they believe and how ultimately how they behave.

In all situations of significance, leaders emerge. Why people choose to follow is a topic studied by many, but in my experience, it comes down to three qualities:

- Trust
- Caring
- Competence

## Trust

People want and need to trust their leaders. A breach of trust, perceived or real, can cause irreparable damage. The process of building trust varies by individual. Integrity can be faked, but not for long. People are attracted to and will follow a leader who is genuine. Authenticity in leadership counts...a lot.

# Caring

There are various versions of the quote "they don't care what you know until they know how much you care." People want to know their leaders have their best interest at heart. It's not about hugs and air kisses in the workplace, it's about humans caring about humans and acting accordingly.

# Competence

Competence may seem like a no-brainer but believe it or not, intelligent people can actually disagree on this one. There are those who believe they can only be led by someone who has more degrees, more years of experience, and more knowledge of a specific business. Every business needs subject matter experts, but they are not always the best people to lead the organization. The best leaders are willingly followed because of their ability to create a shared vision. If a leader motivates others to collaborate, share knowledge, and excel, he or she is a competent leader.

> "Just as beauty is in the eyes of the beholder...leadership is in the eyes of the led."
>
> —Kent Thiry

# *Connection Counts*

Individuals want to be seen *and* heard. Feeling valued is a basic human need, and humans will be more productive if they know their efforts are noticed. There are many stories of leaders who crossed the line and got too close with their team, but more often than not employees leave companies because they feel invisible.

Listening is a skill that comes naturally to some and that can be learned by all. Giving your undivided attention and listening deeply allows you to determine not just the words but the tone and intent. It's not so much about needing to gain agreement or be right; it's about being heard and understood. Failing to sincerely listen is the fastest way to sabotage a relationship with your team and lose good people.

Be present. This means more than just showing up. Being present means being completely engaged in what's going on around you. It's sitting knee to knee or across a table making sustained eye contact. There is nothing worse than getting someone's partial attention, or worse, having a conversation where you walk away realizing you were never looked in the eye. Ten minutes of high-quality time can have far more impact that an entire hour when you are preoccupied or just barely engaged. The gift of your time and attention can do much to improve your connection with your team. In this case it really is about quality over quantity.

If you have a large number of people in your lane, it's important to monitor the amount of quality contact you have with each of your reports. Depending on individual job roles and personalities, the amount of interaction can vary greatly. In the absence of tracking, it's possible some of the less assertive members of your team will be shortchanged. Whatever method of tracking you choose to put in place, review the data regularly and make adjustments if you notice you are failing to have high-quality conversations with any member of your team on a regular basis. It will keep you engaged and send the right message to your team.

## This Really Happened...

I had a boss once who always wanted everyone to know how busy he was. I found it frustrating because it was so difficult to get his attention. He prided himself on being accessible and it is true he almost always answered his cell phone within two rings. Unfortunately he answered even when he was in the middle of meeting with others. He would whisper hello as if doing his best not to disturb someone, making me feel that I had interrupted something crucial and most likely irritating the people he was meeting with. My learning here helped me form my number-one telephone rule, which is "Don't answer the phone if you aren't prepared to give the caller your full attention." It's always better to let the call go to voice mail than make the caller feel slighted and unimportant.

# *The Art of the Apology*

When you screw up admit it; apologize, and mean it. If your apology is perceived as insincere it will do more damage than good. Expressing honest accountability for missteps and errors is an essential leadership skill. Failing to own up to an error is the quickest way to lose credibility and credibility is one of the top attributes people want in a leader. Failure to acknowledge a mistake doesn't mean others don't see it. Ignoring it tends to make an error more noticeable and a leader appear arrogant.

Apologizing shouldn't be easy. Admitting you are wrong will always have an emotional charge. Here are a few tips to help master the art of owning up to a mistake and ultimately make it less difficult.

## Do

- Be timely.
  - o If you wait too long, the impact and authenticity is diminished.
- Be direct and concise.
  - o This not the time for rambling or backpedaling. Get the words out.
- Acknowledge the impact of your error.
  - o Don't just say what you did wrong. Tell the recipient of the apology you

understand the consequences of your mistake and how it impacted them.

- Choose words with strength and integrity.
  - o Speak the truth with clarity and simplicity.

# Don't

- Be a serial apologizer.
  - o Like antibiotics, apologies lose effectiveness with overuse. Apologize thoughtfully and with discretion.
- Be defensive.
  - o Saying "I'm sorry but" can come across as making excuses or worse appear as an attempt to shift the blame for your actions. An apology is invalidated if it isn't accompanied with sincere acceptance of accountability. Resist the urge to explain.
- Apologize preemptively to cover your back.
  - o Rushing to apologize as a self-protective strategy is rarely successful and almost always transparently self-serving. Say you're sorry because you mean it, not to make yourself look good.
- Fail to learn from your mistake.
  - o Nothing diminishes the value of an apology like a repeat offense.
- Dwell on it.
  - o Make a sincere apology and move on. A continual reference back to the incident

is distracting and unnecessary. Move forward.

Authenticity is especially important when apologizing. If you aren't comfortable with it, spend some time practicing what you will say. Preparing a draft of your remarks in advance can ensure you say what you intended to say. You never want an apology to appear rehearsed or insincere, but spending a few minutes reviewing the key points can save a lot of heartache down the line. Exhibit your willingness to surrender the need to be right. Sincerity is essential. An insincere apology does more harm than no apology.

"A genuine apology emphasizes compassion for the wronged party, not redemption for the offender."

—John Kador

"When you realize you've made a mistake, make amends immediately. It's easier to eat crow while it's still warm."

—Dan Heist

# Pushing Back

Some rules were made to be broken. Note the word *some*. There are things that should be nonnegotiable, but for the most part, that level of rigidity should be reserved for issues of safety and integrity. This is not intended to provide an excuse to not do the right thing. The point is that true leaders push back, ask questions, and yes, question authority.

In the life of an organization, rules are made for a variety of reasons, but over time with changes in technology and leadership a reevaluation of processes needs to be a part of every healthy company. It's limiting when a company becomes so large and holds fast to the "way we've always done things". Being flexible, being nimble is a critical trait of successful leaders.

Pushing back is risky and is always easier if those at the very top of the organization embrace the concept of continuous improvement. People who are always questioning rules can be pegged as troublemakers. In my experience, if a rule or policy is frequently being questioned, there is probably something about it that needs reevaluation. Leaders should be asking "What is the evidence that this policy is still relevant, and does it continue to add value to our mission or even just the task at hand?"

Like apologizing, pushing back is also an art. You have to choose when, where, and how you push. If you push back too often, you are likely to be tuned out as a chronic complainer. If you never find a reason to question a policy or process, you are probably overlooking improvement opportunities for both you and your organization.

"The reasonable man adapts himself to the world; the unreasonable one persists in trying to adapt the world to himself. Therefore all progress depends on the unreasonable man."

—George Bernard Shaw

# Resistance Is Futile

Considering you just read a section encouraging leaders to push back and question authority, this statement may seem like a contradiction. The truth is, organizations must change and grow to remain competitive. The time and energy spent resisting change can devastate a company, especially when attempting to integrate teams.

In my early days as a dialysis nurse, I was, appropriately, quite the rule follower. I would resist any change in policy for fear it would impact the quality of patient care. One day I realized that the rapidly developing technology alone would require ongoing adjustment to policies, procedure, and rules and that a huge part of my job was to manage the change. I mark it as one of the pivotal moments in my journey from manager to leader. It was liberating when I realized that my role was to lead the change and guide and support my teammates through the process.

Fighting every change that comes along takes a lot of energy. It's actually much easier to be open to it. In a way it's like the story of the boy who cried wolf. If you constantly question and fight every change, you run the risk of having your opinions discounted. If you express a genuine willingness to consider new ideas, you are more likely to be heard if you need to push back because it's the right thing to do.

As a veteran of both successful and failed integrations, I would never make light of the difficulty of organizational change. In my experience people react negatively if they believe they are being asked to change simply for the sake of change. Transparency is incredibly important when asking our teams to stretch and grow. If they understand the "why" of a situation, the "how it gets done" becomes evident to all.

## This Really Happened...

In the midst of the toughest integration of my career, I came across a lovely picture of a curvy country road with the following caption:

> *"A bend in the road is not the end of the road unless you fail to make the turn."*

I purchased it for my office wall and sent desk-sized versions to all eighty administrators and directors in my division. Many factors played into the failure of that integration, and a few years later a number of us ended up at working for DaVita. Like veterans of the same war, we share a bond and a few scars. One day I walked into the office of one of those teammates and she pointed out the picture on her desk. She thanked me for the wisdom and support the picture represented during that time and said, "I'm so glad we both made the turn and ended up changing to the same lane!"

# *Metrics Matter*

Why talk about metrics in a book about leadership? Because good leaders care about the fulfillment of their team, and fulfillment in work is directly linked to knowing what we do matters. Ideally a high percentage of things we spend our time on will be purposeful and measurable. It is one thing to say your work is important and you are doing a good job, but having the data to prove it is essential to ongoing team motivation. We let our team know what we think is important by what we pay attention to, what we talk about, and what we measure. This leads to the discussion of goals versus budgets.

## Goals

There's a saying that goals that aren't written down are just wishes. Putting pen to paper or marker to flip chart is important. Write it down to make it real. A year out you don't want to be sitting around the table with your team trying to remember what you said you would accomplish. The leader's role is not only to guide the team through goal setting but also to ensure that the goals set are kept in the forefront of the dialogue throughout the year.

There are multiple methods of goal setting. You can find fancy goal boards, online tools, and a variety of templates. In my experience the biggest mistake people make is setting too many goals. Keep it simple at three to five. Committing to a small number of relevant goals elevates the importance of choosing wisely but also reinforces the value of each goal. Resist the urge to set a goal for everything you measure. Keep it simple and save the line-by-line targets for budgets.

Writing it down is important, but saying it out loud in front of your peers greatly increases personal commitment. At the end of a goal-setting session it's a worthwhile practice to go around the table and ask each member of the team to verbalize their agreement and commitment to the goals. This is one area where relentless repetition is desirable. Strong leaders model commitment to the team's goals by keeping them in the forefront of the conversation all year long. It becomes part of the team's fabric resulting in absolute clarity.

> "The reason most people never reach their goals is they don't define them or ever seriously consider them as believable or achievable. Winners can tell you where they are going, what they plan to do along the way, and who will be sharing the adventure with them."
>
> —Denis Waitley

# Budgets

A budget is simply a list of all planned expenses and revenues. If that's true, why is budget season the most dreaded of all for managers? My goal here is not to discuss the various methods and models—that's someone else's book—but to highlight the leader's role in the development and execution.

Depending on the size of your organization, many hands may touch your budget before and after your input. Creating an aggressive but achievable budget is the desired outcome. The leader's role is to see that it's accomplished without causing major turmoil for the team or worse ending up with a budget they believe impossible and won't own. While budgeting is clearly a business process, the art of leadership is critical throughout. A well-planned budget is a beautiful thing, and hitting it can be a source of team pride, Agreeing to something overaggressive, not based in reality, may temporarily get your own boss off your back but will almost always de-motivate your team ("What difference does it make—we don't stand a chance of making our budget anyway.") Conversely, sandbagging or setting super-easy targets can cost you credibility.

Whatever the process, the number one thing the team will notice is the level of leader involvement. Mistakes happen, stuff slips by. It's much easier to live with a bad line item on a budget for a year if the team knows their leader was involved, fought the good fight, and tried to get it right. Leader engagement always matters but never more so than at budget time.

"Our goals can only be reached though a vehicle of a plan, in which we must fervently believe and upon which we must vigorously act. There is no other route to success."

—Stephen A. Brennan

# Leaders Behaving Badly

Leaders are human and therefore imperfect. We all are. Unfortunately, sometimes leaders do behave badly, and the consequences for the team in their line of fire can be devastating.

How leader behavior is dealt with depends heavily on the culture of the organization. Ideally there is a structure in place that calls for formal and informal feedback for each member of the management team. Confident leaders ask for feedback before it's forced upon them.

Yearly 360 reviews with a coach to support the leader through the process is a best demonstrated practice. To obtain useful information, participants require reasonable assurance they will be safe from retaliation. There are many different data-gathering tools with varying levels of complexity, but a simple survey with an opportunity for comments is a great starting point. The success of the process is highly dependent on the emotional maturity of the participants, both the leader and those providing the information.

A solid process for feedback to leaders also provides valuable data to let leaders know what they are doing right. A skilled coach will assist the leader to be open to the feedback and develop a plan that will ultimately be shared with the participants. It's incredibly powerful when post 360 leaders speak honestly about the feedback identifying strengths as well as the areas they can improve.

Being cognizant that even the very top leaders are human is important. It's reasonable to expect more from them, but not perfection. Sometimes bad behavior means a leader must leave, especially if the offense implies a breach of integrity. In others cases it can be a powerful growth experience that results in a change in behavior that benefits all stakeholders.

"Courage is what it takes to stand up and speak;
courage is also what it takes to sit down and listen."

—Winston Churchill

# Case Studies

Compare two situations and the ultimate cost.

Leader # 1

Behavior

- Harsh communication. Routinely lashed out and belittled her team, especially in public. Never took accountability for her actions. Whenever individuals on team succeeded at something, she took credit and never acknowledged the individual privately or publically.

- Alcohol abuse. Was the first to the bar at company functions, consistently leading to intoxication, magnifying her bad behavior.

- Loss of team confidence. Her team of solid performers was quickly losing faith in the organization, as the treatment they received did not align with the company's core values.

Action

One of her direct reports had the courage to take their concerns to the CEO. He knew he was risking retaliation and possibly loss of employment but decided he couldn't continue with the status quo. The CEO engaged in a discreet fact-finding mission and quickly determined there was cause for concern. The leader was informed that she would be given the chance to repair her relationship with her team, but she understood that measurable change was an absolute requirement to remain with the organization. A tough couple of months ensued for everyone. A coach was brought in to assist the team in communicating what they needed from the leader The feedback was accepted and a marked change occurred. The opportunity for reflection led the leader to determine she had an addiction to alcohol. She sought help that led to a marked change in her personal and professional relationships. Today she continues to be a successful executive and contributor to her company's success.

Leader # 2

Behavior

- Sexual harassment. A high-ranking executive known to "go way back" with the CEO crossed the line of propriety with several female employees. All had satisfactory work records but were promptly given corrective action for poor performance after making a complaint to human resources.

- Grandstanding. When results were good this leader took all the credit; when things went wrong he blamed his team.

- Lack of integrity. He used company resources to transport his children to and from his ex-wife's home five hundred miles away. He directed his finance director to bend the rules of accounting to insure positive financial reports.

Action

Over a period of three years, three small settlements were paid to clerical level teammates, and ultimately a six-figure settlement was made to a management-level female whom he attempted to fire after she rebuffed his advances. The CEO continued to maintain he was a "good man" and moved him to other divisions of the company. The reputation of the company, the CEO, and the human resources team suffered greatly and negatively impacted their ability to recruit quality executives.

In each of the above cases an opportunity existed to model strong leadership behaviors. Contrast the action and lack of action of each CEO and the ultimate outcomes. Dealing with bad behavior is never easy, but with courage and integrity the end result can be increased credibility. Ignoring or relocating the problem does a disservice to everyone involved.

"Leadership is a human skill. In order to become a better leader you first have to become a better person."

-Kent Thiry

# *Best Boss Ever*

Most of us can immediately name our best boss ever. In our team workshops, I often ask each team member to talk about a time in their work life when they were the most productive. While the details of their story may differ, a commonality in the description almost always includes positive comments about the person who was their boss. Certainly the work you do and the relationships with coworkers are important in achieving fulfillment, but the leader sets the tone.

Below are the top attributes and behaviors people want in a leader:

- Integrity
- Respect
- Intelligence
- Open-mindedness
- Clarity of vision

## This Really Happened...

I have been blessed with a couple of great bosses in my career, but when pressed for a best ever I have to choose Howie Lewin. Part of what constitutes a great boss–direct report connection is where the individuals are in the cycle of their careers. I remembered Howie from my last year at Vivra, but my exposure to him was limited. I only knew he came from an Ivy League background and that our CEO thought highly of him. In the evolution of the dialysis industry, executives came from two distinct sources. Initially all the operating VPs came up though the ranks like me. You proved you could manage one clinic, then ten, and ultimately a full division of centers. When Kent Thiry entered the industry, he expressed how much he valued those of us with operating experience but gradually introduced the possibility of bringing in talent from outside health care to strengthen the executive team. Initially the non-dialysis-trained executives were put in charge of everything except clinic operations. Years later when I got a call from Howie asking me to help him with a problem he had in the state of Georgia, I was surprised to hear he was a group vice president running several divisions of DaVita (one third of the company). After all, what did a pure business guy know about clinic operations?

I had recently left Fresenius Medical Care after a very difficult two years. I was considering a complete career change but needed to make a living while I figured things out. I came to DaVita offering my assistance to any clinic in trouble. I was working with the team of one of those clinics in Northern California when I got the call from Howie. He had thirty clinics in big trouble all in the state of Georgia. I traveled to Atlanta expecting to help out for a few weeks and then return to some type of consulting role. I ended up staying involved over a year.

Working with Howie was like coming home. He gave me the authority I needed to be effective but allowed me enough access to him when I needed advice. He made it clear he valued my opinions and skills and never appeared judgmental when I had questions. He is highly intelligent, one of the smartest people I've ever known, but never treated me as if he thought I was stupid. On the few occasions we disagreed, he allowed me to speak my piece without retribution. In the end whether he moved to my position or not, it really didn't matter because I knew I had been heard. I valued his opinion, and knowing my view was considered I would support his final decision without reservation. It was possibly the most productive time of my life. I learned that having trust and mutual respect with my boss created an environment ripe for me not just to get work done but also to thrive. Creativity blooms in the absence of fear. I was disappointed when Howie was reassigned and later left DaVita, but I know my time in his group made be a better leader. It also left me with great clarity regarding what I need from a boss to do my best work, and for that I am thankful.

# Leaders of Teams

There are common attributes between leaders of individuals and leaders of teams, but being the leader of a team requires additional skills and qualities. A team is made up of individuals, but the synergy formed when a team comes together forms a distinctive dynamic. Team members learn to interact and deal with the day-to-day challenges of their job. When crisis occurs the leader and team members are stressed to new levels. Sometimes a serious crisis will mark the beginning of the end for a team. Conversely a challenge may be met with strength and integrity and the team emerges with a reinforced commitment to their compelling purpose.

## This Really Happened...

Suzette Quilay was the nurse administrator of a busy dialysis clinic in Sacramento, California. Due to an overflow of patient census, the team needed to treat a few patients each Monday, Wednesday, and Friday evening. The staff took turns picking up the extra evening shifts and Suzette, though not required to do so, took her turn as the RN in charge. It was on one of those evening shifts that disaster happened.

The staff of dialysis clinics routinely prepare for all types of emergencies with a focus on safe evacuation of patients who are connected via needles and blood tubing to a big piece of machinery. The normal disconnection process takes five to ten minutes followed by a period of holding pressure on the needle sites to stop the bleeding that can take another ten to fifteen minutes. An emergency procedure called "cut and clamp" is part of the initial training process of every new nurse and technician, and clinics are required to repeat the process with patients at least quarterly. Machines are stopped, each blood line is clamped a few inches from the needle site, and the tubing is cut just above it. The patient abandons a couple hundred cc's of blood left in the tubing still connected to the machine but in seconds are free to exit a building that for whatever reason is suddenly deemed unsafe. In most clinics the practice sessions take on the air of a grade-school fire drill. Fortunately for all involved it's very rarely used.

One spring evening, two days before Suzette was scheduled to leave for a vacation in Canada, the preparation paid off. Suzette was the only RN in the building with three technicians monitoring several patients connected to dialysis machines. There were no ancillary teammates in the building. The physicians, social workers, dietitians, and clerical staff were all gone for the day. An alert tech noticed something was off, stepped outside, and saw smoke coming out of the roof of the multistory building. Suzette and team went into to action, and with total cooperation and assistance from their patients everyone arrived safely in the parking lot within minutes. By the time they reached the sidewalk and the fire department arrived, the building was completely engulfed in flames. In those critical minutes every member of the team and even some patients exhibited extraordinary leadership. It was a beautiful moment when solid training and humanity came together to save lives. And as the building disappeared before their eyes, with many of their belongings including purses and wallets still inside, the survivors stood together and took in the enormity of how their lives had changed in an instant.

Suzette's leadership definitely set the tone for a great result that evening, but the next several months provided continuing opportunities and challenges. Unlike a retail business, a dialysis clinic can't just close. There were over a hundred patients expecting to show up for treatment over the next two days in a building that, along with their medical records, had burned to the ground. The patients and twenty plus employees across Sacramento watched in shock as they saw the building in flames on the late evening news.

In the short term a command post was set up at a nearby hotel. Working through the night, regional teammates with access to DaVita's electronic records were called in to retrieve the patient contact data, and the clinic team set about phoning every patient to assure them all was well and to ask them to be patient as the team figured out where they would dialyze until the building could be replaced—if the building could be replaced.

In the next twenty-four hours they created a plan that a day earlier would have seemed impossible to execute. Every DaVita clinic in the area had a waiting list. Every shift, every day, was listed as full. The local administrators sat down together and collaborated until a solution could be determined. The patients were triaged and the most critical were sent to the hospital for one treatment.

The displaced team broke into three groups and took over the space of the three nearest clinics at night. Transportation and scheduling issues were complex and required a skill set similar to that of an air traffic controller. By weekend all were back in one of the three centers, and Suzette was managing at three different locations. She canceled her trip to Canada (without being asked) and spent the next months working nights with her team, moving from place to place, re-creating medical records but mostly providing support for her displaced employees. The challenge was big. It was a situation ripe for conflict between her team members and the staff of the centers where they were being hosted. Conflicts did occur, but through it all Suzette never ceased being a role model of for her team. She is a soft-spoken leader whose strength emanates from her core.

It was a glorious day when they moved into their new clinic, built in record time, directly across the street from the old site. The entire team was honored for its bravery, and yes, many people pulled together during the difficult months; but the foundation for all the acts of leadership that occurred was laid well before the building burst into flames. The culture of excellence and spirit of collaboration modeled by Suzette laid the groundwork for all that came after. We never know when or how our integrity will be tested. In a different culture the technicians might have bolted for the door to save themselves but not this team on this night. They were ready to step up and do the right thing. They were well prepared by the quiet strength and values of their leader.

"Never doubt that a small group of thoughtful, committed citizens can change the world. Indeed, it is the only thing that ever has."

—Margaret Mead

# Communicate with Clarity

Take a position and communicate it. Your team should never have to wonder where you stand on issues that impact them. Playing it safe to avoid confrontation on matters of importance is a sure way to lose credibility.

Thoughtful, honest communication is rarely a mistake. Even if you end up on the wrong side of an issue, you will retain the respect of your team and peers for showing the courage to thoughtfully speak your mind.

Humans process information differently. Some assess a situation rapidly and seem to be immediately confident of their stance. Others take more time to consider all the facts carefully before making a decision. In either case solid leadership is in play. It's a failure of leadership to resist taking a side until it's absolutely clear which will be the politically safe viewpoint. Weak leaders try to stay neutral until it's clear what's safe. Courageous leaders take a stand when it counts.

Outstanding leaders should be able to stand before their team and say what they stand for and what they want the impact of their efforts to be. Call it sharing a vision or just clear communication, it comes down to understanding the values and decision-making process of the leader. Whether a formal document or a conversation, the message needs to be clear. Communicating clearly and relentlessly is an essential attribute of a strong leader.

"The single biggest problem in communication is the illusion that it has taken place."

—George Bernard Shaw

# *Perspective*

How we view any situation is seen through the filter of our perspective, a valid view of the world formed over time based on our life experience. Conflict is heightened when we are unwilling to consider an alternate view. Simply taking a minute to question your current perspective can lead to assuming the best of intent instead of judging those around you.

If we are aware that there are many different perspectives for any given situation, we are more inclined to consider things through the eyes of others.

## This Really Happened...

In 2004 DaVita purchased Gambro. Several members of the DaVita Hilton Group, a unit that consisted of vice presidents and above, had lived though the failed Vivra-Gambro integration and carried the scars of feeling not only unwelcome but also devalued. We knew what it felt like to be treated like the enemy as we attempted to join the Gambro team. Years later when we found ourselves on the acquiring side of a merger, we committed to bringing the best of both companies together to build a bigger and stronger organization. I feel comfortable saying "we" because a group of us actually discussed how we were uniquely qualified and motivated to make the integration a positive experience for our new teammates from Gambro. Our CEO committed a huge amount of resources to the integration and stayed personally involved throughout the process. I was personally committed, and when things got tough I reminded myself of how I would want to be treated if I were an acquired executive thrown into the DaVita culture.

I hit a trouble point at the first post-integration nationwide meeting (a gathering of about two thousand clinic administrators and other managers). In previous years I always had some involvement in the meeting planning and at the very least as a member of the Hilton group was given a preview of the big-agenda items and asked to weigh in on any major issues. I arrived at this meeting having very little data about what was to come. It became obvious to me that every single VP selected to be on stage or have any part in leading the activities was a former Gambro executive. The old DaVita VPs were not involved in anything at all. I was surprised but reminded myself of my commitment to the integration and that I trusted the wisdom of our CEO.

One portion of the agenda seemed to be blocked out. Members of the Hilton Group were told to report to the door of the room of their assigned break-out session where they would be given further instructions. There was an air of secrecy that seemed to exclude everyone except a few of the new VPs. I didn't react but felt increasingly uneasy as the meeting progressed. I arrived at my assigned room and was met by Dave and Angie, both from the Gambro side. I was told that my job throughout the break-out session was to guard the door. I was not to let anyone in or out after the two-hour session began. I sought clarification since I knew from experience many in the room would seek a bathroom break. I was told no, they could not leave, and if they insisted on it my job was to absolutely block them from reentering the room. I tried again to find out what the big secret was, reasoning that if I understood what was going on I would be better able to perform my duties. I hit a wall and was told no. I was not part of the planning team and therefore not privy to the information.

At that point I was angry. I didn't say anything but took up my post at the door. My head was pounding. *Who do they think they are? I am a VP with this company and suddenly I am no longer trusted with confidential information?* Similar negative thoughts festered in my head as the presentation began. I did my duty and blocked the door. I controlled my feelings and did not share them with anyone, but I was angry and felt excluded.

It turned out to be a team building exercise where the participants broke into groups and were presented with a bicycle that required assembly. Hundreds of nurse managers worked in groups of four to assemble the bikes. It became obvious that some were provided with tools and some weren't. A large amount of collaboration was required to complete the task, but they did it. A debrief session began, and people called out what they'd learned about the need to share information and tools and importance of sharing information. All in all it was a fun exercise to watch, and though I had let go of some of my anger I was still wondering what the heck the big secret was.

As the session seemed to be winding down, the facilitator reviewed what everyone had learned and asked the group what impact the exercise would have on the day-to-day operation at their clinics back home. The room was quiet, and finally one brave soul spoke up and said, "Not very much". She went on to talk about how with patients on site there was a true sense of urgency to get the machines set up correctly, and putting a bike together was just not the same thing. The facilitator then asked, "What if your customer for this bike was outside the door? How would that change your viewpoint?" Right on cue the doors opened and in marched a group of wide-eyed children with numbers in their hands. They seemed as surprised to see a room full of people standing next to a bunch of new bicycles as we all were to see the children. The numbers were assigned to specific bikes, and the room filled with excitement and tears as the children found their bikes. They turned out to be a group of underprivileged children on an outing with a local service group. They had no idea they would each receive the gift of a new bicycle that day. It was an amazing experience for all. As the room cleared I thanked Dave for planning such an amazing event and asked them why the secrecy with all the VPs. He answered that they wanted to tell as few people as possible so we could all experience the surprise of the beautiful moment when the kids walked into the room. My perspective shifted in an instant. I felt terrible judging my new teammates and embarrassed by all my negative thoughts about being excluded.

The lesson learned was about the power of perspective. I went into the session sure there was a plan to exclude all of the former DaVita VPs. I came away full of gratitude that I worked for a company that created a wonderful service project and provided us the experience of seeing the shining faces of the children at the moment they realized the extent of their good fortune. One actually said, "This is my first lucky day, *ever!*" It was an emotionally charged afternoon.

Most importantly, I knew my new teammates had been thoughtful enough to try to protect my experience and allow me that special moment of surprise. I gained a new perspective, recommitted to personally serve and support the integration, and reminded myself to always assume the best of intent from my peers.

"To laugh often and much, to win the respect of intelligent people and the affection of children, to earn the appreciation of honest critics and endure the betrayal of false friends, to appreciate beauty, to find the best in others, to leave the world a bit better, whether by a healthy child, a garden patch, or a redeemed social condition; to know even one life has breathed easier because you have lived. This is to have succeeded!"

—Ralph Waldo Emerson

# Diversity

Diversity in leadership or the ability to be open to diversity in your team is a key area of a leader's development. In the same way some people are born introverts and others extroverts; some naturally gravitate towards the creation of a diverse group while others almost unconsciously choose to bring in talent just like them.

Creating a diverse team is about so much more than race and gender. Companies track the number of minority hires, but that does not necessarily lead to a diverse workforce. Gender and race are just part of the equation. Discrimination can be subtle and difficult to track. The challenge is to create a team that has enough shared values to work well together but that's not so homogeneous that the members see the world through exactly the same filter.

There is no magic bullet—the key is awareness. Periodically ask questions that will reveal if diversity or lack of it exists in your team. Areas to notice include the following:

- Average Age
  - Is everyone about the same age?
  - Is there representation of multiple generations in the group?
- Education
  - Does a bias exist for graduates of certain schools?

- o Do the team members come from a variety of educational experiences?
- Marital Status
  - o Is there a preference for single or married employees?
- Parental Status
  - o Are potential team members discounted if they have children?
  - o Does everyone on the team have children, causing a childless person to feel left out?
- Background
  - o Is everyone from families of similar income levels?
  - o Would someone from a family of a drastically different income than the group norm feel welcome?
- The Big Ones
  - o Race
  - o Religion
  - o Sexual Orientation

The items listed above are all things to notice and consider. It never makes sense to hire someone just because they are a diverse hire to meet a quota. In the end it's about periodic, thoughtful consideration of the issue. High-functioning teams have the ability to honestly assess the diversity of their group and identify potential blind spots and areas of bias. It's the role of the leader to continually monitor the group's level of awareness and ask the tough questions.

# This Really Happened...

Having worked in California for the bulk of my career, I consider myself one of the least racist people you could meet. I grew up in Fresno, attended school with many different ethnic groups, and have been responsible for teammates all over California's richly diverse population. In my mind I'm color blind. I'm not ignorant to the fact that racism exists, but all of my life I've felt most comfortable in an ethnically diverse group.

One day in my own home I was jolted into a new level of awareness. It was a summer weekday afternoon. I was home because that morning a workman had just completed installing our new on-demand water heater. With the work complete and the bill paid, I decided to spend some time in the backyard swimming pool with my three-year-old grandson, Jack. I live in a nice, middle-class neighborhood. With the weeks of 100-degree-plus temperatures in Fresno, a pool is more necessity than luxury. We were laughing and talking, and I thought I noticed an odd smell but it didn't really register. After a few minutes I heard a voice calling out near the front side gate. I'm not one to go out in public in my swimsuit and Jack couldn't swim so I hurried out of the pool, placed Jack on the steps with orders not to move, and with a towel wrapped around my waist poked my head around the side of the house to see what was going on. A worker from the gas company was standing there by our gas meter. I continued to look back and forth nervously between Jack and the worker so I could be ready to bolt if he took a tumble in the pool. I asked the worker what he needed. He took a long look at me and then said, "Is your husband home?" At that point I bristled because immediately I assumed he was making a sexist assumption. I said, "*I'm* the homeowner; what do you need?" I was nervous about Jack's safety and irritated at the worker for not getting to the point, not to mention self-conscious about the fact that I was in a swimsuit. He started telling me the neighbors had complained about a gas leak and he thought it was coming from our house. I told him I needed to get my grandson out of the pool and throw on some clothes and I would meet him out front.

When I met him out front, he showed me where the gas line connection was broken—most likely by the workers who were there earlier to install the water heater. By now the smell of gas was everywhere. He proceeded with the repair but told me for safety purposes that he would need to come in the house before he left to check all of our pilot lights. The conversation was very businesslike. I left him there to do his work. Back inside the house I told my mom, who lives with me, what was going on. After a while the gas company employee knocked on the door and asked permission to come in and check the pilot lights. My mom was sitting in her chair in the living room and conversed with him a bit. When he finished I walked him to the front door and thanked him for helping fix the problem. I noticed our ending conversation was much warmer than our initial contact.

When I went back in the living room, my mom said, "Did you see what happened?" I had no clue what she was talking about. She told me she noticed he was visibly nervous when he first came in the house. As he checked the pilot attached to our fireplace, he stopped and looked for a very long time at one of the 5 x 7 pictures on the mantle. It was a framed wedding photo of my good friends Theresa and Mitchell. After he studied their likeness, his shoulders relaxed and he became more talkative. It took her a minute to figure it out, and then it hit her. Theresa and Mitchell are black, as was the worker. Until she told me what she witnessed I truly hadn't noticed his skin color.

So many thoughts went through my head as I replayed the events of the afternoon. It never even registered that race had anything to do with his reaction to me or his impression of my reaction to him. It was only when he realized we were close enough to a black family to have their picture on our mantle that he was able to relax. I can't possibly know what hurdles he's faced over the years, but I know enough to surmise that some of his customers were unwilling to allow a black man in their home. It may well be that he would have preferred to talk to a man, but it's equally as likely that he read my behavior peeking around the corner of the house as unwelcoming and assumed my glances back and forth were based on a fear of him, not that I was afraid my grandson would slide into the pool.

My learning that day was that no matter how comfortable I am in this multiracial world, it's important to be mindful that the experiences of others have framed their perspective and beliefs that ultimately impact their behaviors. Diversity awareness is a lifelong process.

"I look to a time when brotherhood needs no publicity: to a time when a brotherhood award would be as ridiculous as an award for getting up each morning."

—Daniel D. Mich

# *Accountability*

*I'm accountable.* Together those are two powerful words. Having the emotional maturity to take accountability for your actions, decisions, and ultimate results, whether good or bad, is a sure sign of a seasoned leader. Taking accountability is an acknowledgment of who will stand up and be responsible to guide any given project or area and who will pick up the pieces when things go wrong.

Perhaps the biggest lesson to be learned is the difference between taking accountability and taking the blame. The other is that being accountable doesn't necessarily mean you stand alone.

*ac·count·abil·i·ty*

*noun*

the quality or state of being accountable; *especially*: an obligation or willingness to accept responsibility or to account for one's actions

## This Really Happened...

In 1996 a tragedy occurred in the Vivra dialysis clinic in Bakersfield, California. Darlene was the long-time nurse administrator, and she reported to our newest regional director, Sean Graham. She was a timid person and I knew she preferred reporting to a female director, but Sean was absolutely the right person to be promoted to that director position and I truly believed he had the potential to make her a stronger leader. I sat down with Darlene before making Sean's new assignment official and asked her to be open to what Sean could teach her. I had known her for years, and it was one of the best conversations we ever had. She had a couple of employees she had long considered underperformers and agreed that she would work with Sean to determine the next step to begin the appropriate progressive disciplinary action. It was a hopeful time in her career. She was ready to step up and deal with the issues she usually shied away from.

I received periodic reports, and in October we all came together for our annual divisional administrators meeting. As the divisional VP I always took advantage of those three-day meetings to speak with as many of the administrators as possible one-on-one. Darlene was at the top of my list to catch up with. She told me things were going well with Sean and that she finally found the courage to discipline Gloria, a long-term teammate. It was a name I'd heard associated with problems over the years, so it made sense she would be one of the first to have issues, as Darlene created a culture of accountability in her clinic. She told me Gloria had been given a final written warning and if she violated another policy her employment would be terminated. There was an energy coming from Darlene that I had never seen before. It wasn't that she was excited at the prospect of firing someone, but it was obvious she was feeling empowered to make the changes needed to improve. I told her I was proud of her and I would look forward to getting progress reports from Sean. It was the last conversation Darlene and I would ever have.

The meeting concluded, and about a week later Sean and I were both in the divisional office. I overheard bits of a phone conversation he had with Darlene. After the call he let me know that Darlene had arranged for the processing of Gloria's final check and that she would be fired the next day. I asked if he would be going to Bakersfield to be there for the termination meeting, and he said no. He'd offered to be there but Darlene said she would just have the charge nurse sit in the meeting as a witness. It's never a good day approving the termination of an employee, but this definitely seemed like the right thing to do and in all our minds it had been a long time coming.

The next day I was in the divisional office alone with my assistant who took the call. It took a minute for me to process what she telling me. Darlene had been shot. I knew I must have heard incorrectly, and at first I was actually irritated that someone would make a joke like that. In minutes the truth sank in. In fact, Darlene did hold the termination meeting with Gloria that morning. At the conclusion she and the charge nurse walked her to the break room to get her belongings out of a locker. In a split second, Gloria pulled a loaded gun out of the locker and shot Darlene in the eye before running out the back door.

I was in my car in within minutes driving the one hundred miles from Fresno to Bakersfield. Cell phones were large, new, and expensive back then, but I had one and made full use of it as I broke all speed laws on Highway 99 driving to the clinic. The clinic staff told me Darlene was dead before I got there, but I held out hope they were wrong. When I arrived the clinic was surrounded with news crews. The medical examiner had just removed Darlene's body. One of the police officers informed me that when they went to Gloria's home to arrest her, she put the gun to her own head and was now on life support. The patients had all been disconnected from the machines, the afternoon shift diverted to other clinics, and each employee appeared to be in some level of shock.

The main thing I remember about the next few days is the energy it took all of us to move forward. I recall calling Sean from the road and suggesting he stop by his home and get some clothes before coming to the clinic. I thought he might need to stay overnight. Little did I know we both would end up being there for weeks.

It was an emotional time for all, and Sean and I worked together to get the clinic operational again. There was no written policy on how to proceed. The California state surveyors showed up within hours. Representatives of OSHA were there the second day. They all wanted to know our "plan." I remember thinking, *I don't have a plan, I'm just trying to hold this place together.* Darlene's family was understandably devastated and for a period of time decided Sean and I were to blame for the shooting. Ex-employees from years before came out of the woodwork to speak on the news about how they had warned Vivra management that Darlene was a weak manager who needed to be removed. For others Darlene took on saint status and they blamed us for not knowing that Gloria was unstable. It was, to say the least, the toughest time of my career.

Support from Vivra clinics came in from all over. The clinic filled with flowers and gifts. Notes of condolence for the remaining team and offers of assistance were plentiful. Kent Thiry, our CEO, came and sat in the clinic grieving with the devastated teammates for several hours. He was the one who stepped in and listened with empathy and caring to the anger of Darlene's family while remaining in full support of the decisions Sean and I made. I was amazed and numb at the same time. A huge amount of assistance came in the form of the Vivra corporate office, which took full responsibility for dealing with all requests from the media, and there were many.

We did everything we could think of to ease the situation. Grief counselors were on site; we pulled our best technicians and nurses from surrounding clinics to backfill the local team. I had a daily phone check-in with my boss at the time David Barry, COO. From our first conversation in my car as I headed into the chaos until the day we attended Darlene's memorial together, he was a solid source of support. I picked him up at the tiny Bakersfield airport to attend the memorial service and to record the first official statement for television news on behalf of Vivra since the shooting.

We spoke privately before we entered the building where the memorial was held. I was beyond emotional exhaustion at that point and questioning every decision I'd made back to the day I signed the document approving Gloria's termination. With none of the teammates around to hear, I finally said out loud what had been the recurring theme in my head. I told him I knew I was ultimately to blame for everything that happened, and I would understand fully if asked for my resignation. He looked surprised and asked me why I thought it was my fault. I rambled on a bit about being the one to approve the termination, about my pushing Darlene to be a stronger leader, and that I was ultimately responsible for everything that happened in the division. While I may not remember his words verbatim, I will never forget the look on his face, the tone of his voice, and the message when he replied. He said, "Yes you are responsible for this, as am I. It's not the same thing as being to blame. We make the best decisions we can with the information we have. You aren't the one who brought a loaded gun to work and pulled the trigger. This was a terrible thing to happen, and you and I are responsible for getting these employees and patients through it. We are accountable for this clinic and together we will continue to do what's needed as long as it's needed." As we walked into the memorial I envisioned Kent, David, Sean, and I standing to together to represent Vivra. It was a vision that provided me great strength over the next difficult weeks.

It took months before things got back to any kind of normal, and many people provided support and assistance along the way. My lessons were many, but most of all I came away understanding accountability and that when things get really tough, shared accountability with colleagues you trust is a beautiful thing.

# *Seasons of Leadership*

Some may say they became leaders by accident, but I contend we always have a choice. Choosing to be a leader for life must be a conscious decision or it is not a true act of leadership. Mistakes will be made, home runs will be hit, and for a time things may settle down. It is all part of the journey and the learning.

In the end, whether we choose to lead or follow (and Leaders for Life will do both) the only true measurement of our success is the impact our actions have on those we lead. Making a positive impact, leaving people and situations better than you found them, is the ultimate mark of leadership. It is sensing when to step aside and let others lead. It is gathering the wisdom and strength to recognize those you've mentored who have surpassed you in ways you never imagined, and basking in the joy of their success.

Leadership is not for the faint of heart. It is challenging, messy, and at times excruciatingly painful. It is having the emotional maturity and open-mindedness to continue to be surprised by the opportunities to serve, teach, and impact the world in all seasons of life. It is the ultimate in fulfillment and satisfies the human need to make a difference. And it is, in my opinion, totally worth it.

"Guided by the belief that our actions have impact well beyond our line of vision, we acknowledge the power of choice, perspective, and accountability."

—Be the Pebble Leadership Coaching for Life

For information on coaching of teams and individuals or to schedule the author for speaking engagements or workshops, contact Be the Pebble at 866 299 1232 or via email at beapebble@gmail.com

# *Credits*

The front cover drawing was originally created over fifteen years ago by my son, **Teddie Lopez**, at the time a high school student. One afternoon he stopped by my office (most likely to ask for money). He sat in the chair across from me waiting for me to get off a lengthy call and in boredom began drawing the picture that I eventually framed and now treasure. Thanks to Mariah for taking it digital.

Illustration—**Mariah Demarco** (talented daughter-in-law), Demarco Design

Back cover photo—**Mark Janzen** (talented son-in-law), Mark Janzen Photography

Thanks for sharing your talent!